Sun gives me power. My dreams are true. I Feel energies. Pray has a lot of powers. Spiritual world is infinity. It has so much to say. Pure love open 4th dimension. Pray is law of attraction. My orha is my power. Algorithm depend on law of magic. I am a master of my soul. My truth makes me bold. My destiny is infinity. Cosmos says me intuition. My wisdom gives me power. A new world is born for me that is 4th dimension. I experience full glory of 4th dimension.

My prayer is full align. I experience the noor. Energy is a food of soul. I express my magic and power. The truth gift me love. I spread my energies like a butterfly. I will have a lot to explore. Wisdom explores our conscious mind.

Spirituality means love. I see the world from different view. My intuition guides me. I have no worries of tomorrow. I will not stop by fear. My prostration connect me to the divine. I make my soul shine.

I am an ocean of love. I commune with the stars. My wisdom is my fortune. I have a energy of loving space. My Prostration uplift my soul. I awaken my inner peace. My energies touch the skies. I hold a lot of energy.

I do everything with the strength of my truth. I have a divine wisdom. I survive with great transformation. My energies are very old. You see the pain in my smile. My soul connected with divine like magnetic poles. The universe gift me powers to see the truth. Weather depend on my mood.

The sky in harmony with me. My love extend my soul. I trust myself. I dive down into the depth of my soul. When I was awaken. I came to hear the voice of spirit. I discover myself in midnights.

I don’t go in search of my destiny. I just struggle to learn humanity. I always gratitude when I see nature. Everything is limitless. Everything is divine. I have a pure faith of God.

My tears refuse to stop each tear carry ocean of pain. My tear heal my wounds. The foundation of my life is love. I welcome the challenges. Love grow my spirit. The purpose of my life is to grow soul.

Divine brought me to my
feet. I hope to the divine for
something new. Miracle
done with years of patience.
My soul feels healing. I seek
answers to my question. I
quiet seat and focus.
Wisdom explores my
conscious mind.

Spirituality is infinity. I
mostly silent and observe.
The ocean of strength behind
my eyes. I feel the essence of
the souls. The more I bow,
the more I get superior,
there is a miracle in divines
worship. The song of my soul
is humanity. The world is so
abundance by miracles.

Marvel mind creates by wisdom. Witches eat my thought. My conscious level increase by wisdom. Matrix work by my thoughts. I am grounded deep to the spirituality. My love gives me strength.

The purpose of life is to serve humanity. Firmament shakes by sigh of an oppressed person. God has accurate wisdom. I put my problems in God hand. Trust God everything happen with a reason. When I saw demon and witches, divine protect me.

Pray heal me. The foundation of spirituality is love, knowledge, and wisdom. Prayer is a source to connect God. The fire of truth save me. I rise from the darkness. Light extended in to my body. Love help me for my spiritual growth. The greatest beauty of bowing is that you whisper with earth is reflected on sky.

I serve my life to the divine.
When I see sky light travel on
sky. My uniqueness is my
strength. I search loneliness
in a root of things. I saw a big
spirit his age is belong to
Adam's century. I have a
pure soul. Angels enter light
in to my body.

People eye zoom in to my eyes. My orha is become bigger with time. Honesty gives you grounded in spirituality. No thought no wishing. All knowledge comes from God. The journey of spirituality has so many treasures. Expect the unexpected.

Listen to the sound of silence, it is the oneness sound. Adventure by love. Love speak for itself. I accept all adventure in to my life. I totally surrender. I have bruise in my body. The reason of bruise is the truth way. When snakes crawl into my veins. I saw aliens.

The purpose of my life is to search God. I feel snakes crawl on my skin. The universe has so many treasures. The needles prick on my skin. I give attention to my spirit. Find your way and trust yourself it will become journey of whole.

The universe plan my journey. Be humble, be kind. Concentrate Magic of silence and the way of silence. Miracle happen by consistency, love, knowledge and wisdom. Helping other is a real spirituality. The highest level of spiritual awakening is miracle.

Go to the deeper essence of anything makes you spiritual. Source is an ocean and human is a drop of ocean with wisdom you can drink whole ocean. When you reach to loneliness and sound of silence. Your journey to source will end up. Loneliness is a depth of anything which is search by our mind. My enlighten start with prostration.

Be patient and believe in consistency. I heal by sharing. Gratitude is a kind of spiritual fulfillment. I walk through dimension. I saw shadows and God name emerge on wall. I feel warm air around me. It's time to big orha again.

The sign of guidance around me everywhere. The new frequency of miracles is very high. I am not scared at all. I nurture and creates space for healing. Source depend on our wisdom. I have the thirsty soul. Spirituality is all about physics fiction.

This journey will become soon reveal. A big miracle is on the way. I saw witches. They eat my energies. My all nights spend with nightmares. An ant appear and disappear on my surrounding. Birds change in to daemon or spirit. I am not ascetic.

Fairies change into butterflies. Law of attraction play an important role in my life but without worship of God you can't do miracles. Daemon and witches give me signs that they are here. Miracle occur when you are good human being.

Good human being are those who follow God guidance. Sometimes birds convert into spirit and sometime spirit convert into birds. I saw a black jaguar type daemon who is belong to the family of protector daemon for dajjal. In my hands a lot of beautiful insects in rainbow color appear which I didn't see any where.

I am in the higher level of consciousness. I love to walk barefoot because the earth give me energy. Everything is possible in spirituality. Spirituality is carry mysterious wounds. Miracles is a gift of God which is revelate by angel for obedient human being.

www.ingramcontent.com/pod-product-compliance
Lightning Source LLC
LaVergne TN
LVHW020547160826
845677LV00015B/4238

* 9 7 9 8 8 4 7 6 6 7 3 4 0 *